Plants & Animals

Consultant: John Stringer BSc

ReD

Welcome to Mad About Science: Plants & Animals!

Do you know what the largest living thing is? Or how a plant feeds itself? Or why you get out of breath when you run? Our planet is alive! From birds to beetles and flowers to ferns, there are over 1.7 million different living things on Earth – and these are just the ones that we know about!

With a range of exciting and fun experiments, amazing fact boxes and colourful illustrations, this book is a complete guide to the living, breathing, moving and growing world around us. Throughout the book, you will find experiments that are great fun and easy to do. Most of the things that you will need for them can be found in your home. Plant seeds can be bought from a garden or DIY centre. Follow the instructions for each experiment carefully and always take care when you are using sharp tools and knives.

If you want to learn about a particular subject, just look it up in the index at the back. Otherwise, simply turn to page 4 and let the fun begin!

Contents

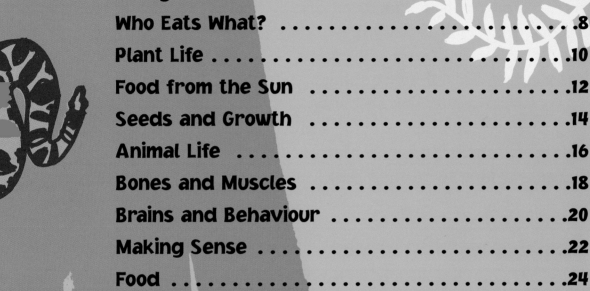

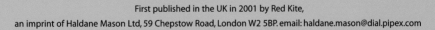

First published in the UK in 2001 by Red Kite,

an imprint of Haldane Mason Ltd, 59 Chepstow Road, London W2 5BP. email: haldane.mason@dial.pipex.com

Copyright © Haldane Mason Ltd, 2001

ISBN: 1-902463-29-3

A HALDANE MASON BOOK

Editor: Kate Latham   **Designer:** Rachel Clark   **Illustrators:** Phil Ford & Stephen Dew   **Educational Consultant:** John Stringer BSc

Colour reproduction by CK Litho Ltd, UK

Printed in the UAE

Picture Acknowledgements

Bruce Coleman Collection 10b, 12, 23, /E & P Bauer 8, /E Bjurstrom 27, /Jane Burton 16, /Alan Compost 20, /Sarah Cook 29, /Christer Fredriksson 24, /Hans Reinhard 4, /Petr Zabransky 15, /Gunter Ziesler 7, 19; **Sydney Francis** 10t; **Science Photo Library** 26.

Note: The experiments described in this book are designed to be safe and easy to carry out at home. The author and publishers can accept no responsibility for any accidents that occur as a result of using the book. If in doubt, consult an adult.

Being Alive

Have you ever stared at the stars and wondered whether life exists on other planets? Well, until humans go to pay a visit or aliens arrive here, you won't know. What you can be sure of, though, is that our planet – Earth – is home to a fabulous variety of living things, from the tiniest bacterium (which can only be seen under powerful microscopes) to the massive blue whale, which is over 30 metres long (that's longer than a swimming pool).

The largest living things on Earth, giant Sequoia trees grow to an incredible 90m high and 30m wide.

What makes something alive?

Scientists have identified and named about 1.7 million different species – or types – of living things, but there are probably many millions more out there which we have yet to discover. Every living thing is made up of tiny 'cells' which work together to form all of the physical body and to carry out the necessary functions for life. You are made of trillions of these cells, including the billions of bacteria that live on your skin and inside your body.

4

Changing world

Most scientists believe that life first appeared on Earth about 3.4 billion years ago, when the planet was already about 1.2 billion years old and still cooling down from the process that made it. The first organisms – or living things – were something like bacteria but, in time, more and more complex organisms appeared. This constant change over time is called evolution, and it's the way that most scientists think life on Earth developed, including the appearance of us humans. It means that species change as they adapt to different conditions. Those that cannot adapt die out – they become extinct.

An amoeba is a very simple life form which lives in water. It is a protist – an organism that consists of only one cell.

The nucleus is the 'brain' of the cell, controlling its functions

Did you know?

What's in a name?

In the 18th century, Swedish botanist Carolus Linnaeus realized that, with all the many different types of animals and plants in the world, there was an urgent need for a method of classifying them – that is, putting them into some sort of order based on how closely related they were.

He worked out a way of naming them, so that every species of living thing would have a name that people would recognize. Each species was given a two–word name in Latin. This was a great improvement because some animals had

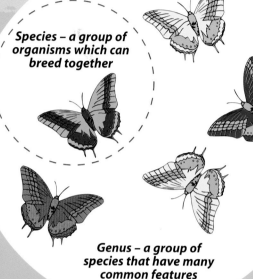

Species – a group of organisms which can breed together

Genus – a group of species that have many common features

names made up of over ten words! The first name showed the group of animals – known as the genus – that the species belonged to (a bit like your surname) while the second name showed the actual species (like your first name). This system is still used by scientists today. Tigers and lions, for example, both belong to the same genus, *Panthera*. But the lion is *Panthera* (genus) *leo* (species), while the tiger is *Panthera tigris*. You, by the way, are formally known as *Homo sapiens* (provided that you are human, of course).

Try this! Grouping together

You will need a collection of coins. Now pick out features – such as the size, shape, and colour – that make some different from others. This is just what Linnaeus would have done when classifying species. Draw up a chart, like a family tree, to divide your coins into groups, where all coins look alike in some way.

You could also try this with a selection of leaves from your garden or the park, grouping them by colour and size.

Amazing fact

Tardigrades, or water bears, are microscopic animals that live among damp leaves in woody areas or in drainpipe gutters on your house. They can 'play dead' for as long as 25 years then, if placed in water, they immediately come back to life. This amazing ability helps them survive the times when their normally wet home is dried out.

Living Places

You could probably describe the sort of area you live in and its surroundings. Are the shops easy to get to? Is there a park nearby? Does the Sun shine a lot, or does it rain all the time? As living things are found just about everywhere on the Earth's surface (and beneath it), their surroundings vary a lot, but they will only be able to survive in habitats or places which provide the food and shelter they need.

Plants and animals survive in environments that vary widely in terms of climate, conditions and resources. They must adapt to cope with their surroundings and to protect themselves.

Try this! Habitat scrapbook

Search through magazines to find pictures of as many different habitats as you can, if possible showing the types of plants and animals found there. Cut the pictures out (get permission first) and make a habitat scrapbook so you can see the world's living places at a glance. Notice the similarities between animals that live in the same types of habitat but in different places, such as the monkeys that live in South America's tropical forests, and those that live in the forests of Africa.

Did you know?

Species of animals and plants can naturally die out (become extinct). But the speed at which this is happening has increased. Why? It's because of human beings – us. As the human population increases (there are now 6 billion people in the world and roughly 150 babies being born every minute) we are using up more of its resources, destroying more habitats, causing more pollution, and changing the climate. Now thousands of animals are threatened. These include important species such as the tiger, panda and gorilla, and many less obvious smaller animals that disappear without us noticing. Plants are threatened as well, and this endangers the animals that rely on these for food, and also us, because humans use many plants as cures for illness and disease.

The tiger will be extinct in five years' time if it is not protected from poachers and loss of habitat.

Amazing fact

The Arctic fox is a great survivor. It can withstand freezing conditions in ice and snow with temperatures as low as −50°C. A thick layer of fat under its skin, and very thick fur, helps to keep the bitter cold out.

African grasslands

No animal lives in isolation; all are linked together. This is true everywhere in the world. For example, look at the dry grasslands of the African savannah. These extremely spacious grasslands are warm all year round, with a dry season during the summer. The soil is too poor for many trees to grow there, but grasses and small bushes can survive. There are animals which eat just plants (herbivores). They feed most of the day because there isn't much goodness in grasses and leaves. Zebras eat the tough top parts of grasses while giraffes, with their long necks, can eat from the few trees. This means that they don't compete for food and all can survive together. Herbivores are tasty meals for the meat-eaters (carnivores), such as lions and hyenas that hunt in packs.

Many species of animals live on the African savannah grasslands.

Who Eats What?

All over the world, people depend on the family and friends around them, especially our near-neighbours. Animals and plants that live in a particular place or habitat are also linked together – often because they eat each other to survive. Humans who live in one place talk of being part of a community. The same is true of animals and plants that share the same habitat.

Owls feed on a wide range of animals, including insects, fish, small birds and mammals, and even young foxes.

Down the chain and through the web

The way that the community interacts with its surroundings – whether it is grassland, a swamp or wherever – forms a relationship called an ecosystem. Essential to the whole operation is the Sun. Sunlight energy flows down to Earth, into plants (which use it to make food, as explained on page 12), and then into the animals that eat the plants, and on into the animals that eat those animals, and so on. The easiest way to describe a who-eats-what relationship is by using what is called a food chain. Take a mouse and a snake. The mouse feeds on grass, and the snake eats mice. The energy from the Sun flows along the chain from grass to snake. Simple? But it's not quite as simple as that. In woodlands, mice eat grasses, but they are also hunted by large birds that might also kill a rabbit (which also eats grass). Foxes also eat mice. And so on. Suddenly, the simple food chain has hundreds of links and has become a food web. This is the easiest way to show how a community forms an ecosystem.

8

Energy from the Sun passes from plants to herbivores and small animals, and then to larger animals in the food chain.

Try this!

Where did it come from?

You will need a pen and paper. Every time you eat something, you find yourself at the end of a food chain. Unless you get eaten by a whale or a lion, of course, in which case you're the second-to-last link in the chain! Make a list of all the foods you have eaten today, and then try to work out the food chain that led to you. For example, a piece of beef comes from a cow that fed on grass that made its own food using sunlight. Or, the cereal that you had for breakfast was probably made from wheat or oats, which are plants and which use sunlight energy to make food, as do vegetables and fruit. Even chocolate comes from a plant – the cocoa plant.

Did you know?

Not all plants and animals are eaten by other species as food. Decomposers are very useful plants and animals which clean up dead animals and plants that haven't been eaten. These species (which aren't actually classified as plants or animals) are the fungi and bacteria that live in the soil and break down dead living things so that they seem to disappear. What they actually do is to release special minerals (such as nitrogen and phosphorus) into the soil. These are soaked up through plant roots, and help the plant to grow and prosper, along with the animals that eat the plant until, eventually, they die and are recycled once again by the decomposers.

Amazing fact

In the ocean's depths, some 2,500m below the surface, it is pitch-black and the water pressure is so high that it would squash you as flat as a pancake. But living things are found here, including giant tube worms up to 3m long. They live around vents, like chimneys, from which hot water gushes, heated by rocks in the Earth's crust. With no sunlight, food chains here are very different from the surface. The hot water contains sulphur. This is used as an energy source by tiny bacteria which then provide food for the tube worms.

Plant Life

Plants will grow wherever there is water and light, and if it is not too cold and windy. Below ground, their roots take in water from the soil which travels up the stem to other parts of the plant. Water helps to keep a plant upright, as you may have noticed when you forgot to water that pot plant. What you may not realize is that, without plants, we humans and all other animals would not survive. Plants are the source of the oxygen in the air, the stuff we need to breathe to stay alive. So, be nice to plants!

Flowering plants

Plants with flowers – also known as flowering plants – are probably the most obvious to us. They're the ones you find in the garden, or a florist, or even in a field of wheat (yes, they have flowers as well, but not very colourful ones). The green leaves use sunlight to make food, while the flowers produce seeds which will eventually grow into new plants. The roots of the plant dig downwards, into the ground, to keep the plant upright. Roots also absorb water and minerals from the soil which are necessary for the plant to make its own food and keep healthy.

A flowering plant, with a single flower head at the top of the stem.

Did you know?

Trees that lose their leaves every autumn are called deciduous trees. The leaves often turn bright colours before they detach themselves from their branch and fall to the ground. It is too cold in winter for the leaves to make any food so the tree loses its leaves for the winter months and makes new ones the following spring.

10

Plants without flowers

There are other types of plants as well. Mosses are tiny plants that generally live in clumps in wet places. Ferns are bigger, but they usually like damp places as well. Both mosses and ferns don't make seeds, like flowering plants. They reproduce by releasing tiny spores – small seeds – into the air. If spores land in the right place, they grow into a new plant.

Conifers are bigger still. These trees, including pine trees and your Christmas tree, do produce seeds but not inside flowers. Instead, they make them inside cones, something you always find lying about when you walk through a pine forest. Conifers usually have very narrow leaves, like needles (in fact, that's what they're called), that they don't lose all at once in autumn. This helps conifers to survive in places that can be dry or very cold, like the great, dark forests of northern Europe.

Conifers and mosses are simple plants which lived on Earth over 400 million years ago; flowering plants followed 250 million years later.

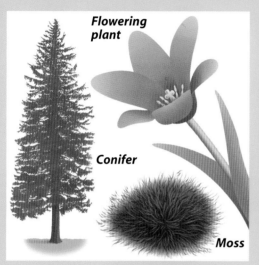

Flowering plant

Conifer

Moss

Amazing fact

Flowering plants form the biggest and most varied group of plants on Earth. There are over 250,000 different species found everywhere from baking deserts to the freezing Arctic.

11

Try this!

Water flow

You will need a jar or glass, some coloured ink or food colouring and a stick of leafy celery. Water moves up a plant's stem along tiny tubes called xylem, which are a bit like drainpipes. To show how this happens, take a stick of celery and ask an adult to trim one end. Put the stem in a jar containing the ink and water, until the celery is standing in at least 5cm of coloured water. Leave it in sunlight for 12 hours. Now, take the celery out of the jar and ask an adult to cut across the celery stick half way along its length. Look at the cut ends. You should see lots of coloured dots (the colour of the ink that you used). These show where the xylem tubes – carrying the coloured water – have been cut in half.

Food from the Sun

Plants can't move, so they can't go looking for food, but they don't have to – they can make their own food without going to the trouble of chasing after wildebeest or going to the supermarket. All it takes is a basic recipe and a few simple ingredients – and, no, you can't do this at home.

Green is good

Food-making happens inside a plant's leaves. Inside each leaf are lots of tiny oval blobs called chloroplasts. Packed inside each of these is a green substance called chlorophyll. Chlorophyll is remarkable because it can actually grab hold of the Sun's energy from sunlight and make use of it. There are only two other ingredients: the gas carbon dioxide (which comes from the air through tiny holes in the leaves) and water, which comes up to the leaves through the stem from the roots. Now, here's the extraordinary bit – the energy trapped by chlorophyll joins together carbon dioxide and water to produce a sugar called glucose. This is packed full of energy that the plant can use. And you make use of it too – every time you eat a banana or any other part of a plant.

12

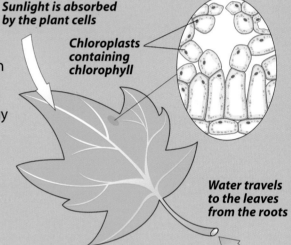

Sunlight is absorbed by the plant cells

Chloroplasts containing chlorophyll

Water travels to the leaves from the roots

Each cell in a plant leaf contains many tiny structures called chloroplasts which are filled with chlorophyll.

Tropical forests

The world's tropical forests lie in a belt around the equator, from central and south America, through Africa, to south-east Asia. If you were standing in one now, you would be hot and sweating, and you might find a few creepy-crawlies running up your leg. The mixture of plenty of sunshine, lots of warmth and water makes it ideal for plant growth. The rich green colour is produced by the chlorophyll in its many different types of plants, which provide homes and food to millions of animal species. The bad news is that these forests are at risk world-wide. As human populations grow, people want to chop down the trees to make money from timber, or clear the forests to create extra farmland.

Try this!

Plant gas

You will need a bowl, a glass or beaker and some pondweed. Fill the bowl with water. Put some pondweed into the jar and fill it with water, right to the top. Immerse the jar carefully in the bowl of water and turn it upside down – still full of water so that no air gets in – to rest the open end of the jar, with the pondweed inside, on the bottom of the bowl. Check that there is no air in the jar. Place the bowl in sunlight and leave for a few hours. You will soon notice bubbles of gas appearing on the leaves of the pondweed. In time these float up to the top of the jar. This is the oxygen that plants produce when they make food for themselves.

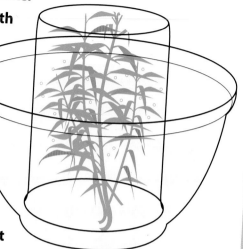

Try this!

Following the Sun

You will need 2 small bowls or half eggshells, a couple of handfuls of seed compost, a packet of cress seeds and a box with a small slit in one side (get an adult to help you with this). Plants grow towards the Sun and you can test this. Take the plastic bowls or half eggshells. Fill each with seed compost. Sprinkle some cress seeds over the compost in each one, and water them carefully. Put one set of seeds in a dark place (such as a cupboard). Cover the other seeds with the box with the slit in the side and place it with the slit facing towards light. Leave the bowls for a week to let the seeds sprout (and don't be tempted to cut the cress seedlings to make sandwiches). What do you see? The seeds left in the dark have grown into plants which are long and skinny with yellowish leaves. They have been struggling to find the light they need to grow. The ones under the box have green leaves, and have grown towards the slit in the box in the search to get out into the sunlight.

Did you know?

Hundreds of years ago, people believed that there were man–eating plants. Fortunately, that's not true. But there are some plants – called carnivorous plants – that gobble up juicy flies and other insects. The Venus fly trap has a particularly nasty surprise waiting for its victims. It has special leaves that work like a spring trap. If a fly lands on the trap, the two halves of the trap snap shut. No amount of struggling can free the poor old fly. Pretty soon the Venus fly trap digests the fly, and the plant mops up its nutritious juices.

13

Seeds and Growth

How many poor, defenceless baby plants have you eaten recently? None at all, you may answer, revolted by the thought. But think again. If you have eaten peanuts, peas, beans, rice, lentils, or even popcorn, baby plants are precisely what have gone into your mouth. All of those foods are seeds, and seeds are created by plants when they reproduce.

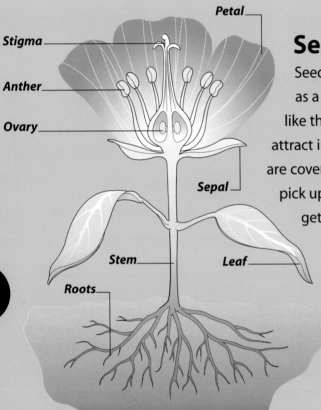

Petal

Stigma

Anther

Ovary

Sepal

Stem

Leaf

Roots

14

Seeds

Seeds are made by flowers. If you were to take a flower such as a lily or tulip and slice it in half lengthways, it would look like this flower. You can see the brightly coloured petals that attract insects. You can also see the anthers that produce and are covered by powdery pollen, one or more sticky stigmas that pick up pollen and the ovary where the seeds develop. Pollen gets shifted from the anther of one flower to the stigma of another by insects visiting to feed on the sweet nectar produced by flowers, and sometimes by the wind. The pollen fertilizes the eggs inside the flower's ovary and soon the ovary – now called a fruit – is bulging with seeds. Each seed is a package containing one baby plant and the food store that will keep it going as it germinates (grows).

How does your garden grow?

Whether they're lilies, oak trees, cabbages or carrots, most of the plants around you grow from seeds. With a bit of luck, if a seed lands on a decent bit of soil it has a good chance of germinating – that is, growing into a new plant. It also needs a reasonable amount of warmth – it won't germinate on a freezing winter day – and plenty of water. The new plant's stem grows up towards the Sun while, sensibly, its roots delve downwards into the soil in search of water. Very soon, if it isn't eaten by a passing rabbit or squashed by your boot, it will produce flowers and seeds of its own.

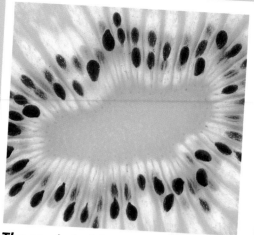

The seeds inside a kiwi fruit.

Did you know?

Plants have many ingenious and necessary ways of dispersing or spreading their seeds – if seeds land too close to their parent, in no time they would be slurping up their parent's water supply. Fruits like strawberries are yummy; animals wolf them down, and the seeds appear from the other end unharmed and nowhere near the parent. Sycamore trees have wing-shaped fruits that spin through the air. Dandelions produce tiny parachutes that simply blow away. Coconuts fall into the sea and wash up on another beach. And some fruits are sticky or hooked – they get caught in animals' fur and spread that way.

Try this! Watching germination

You will need a clean jar or tall glass, 2 sheets of blotting paper or kitchen towel, cotton wool and a bean seed. Normally you can't see germination happening because the seed is buried in the soil. This way you can. Take the jar or glass and line it with the blotting paper or kitchen towel. Loosely fill the inside of the blotting paper with cotton wool. Now put a broad bean seed half way down the jar, between the paper and the glass. Add some water to the cotton wool but do not cover the seed. Put the jar in a dark place (to pretend the seed is underground) and look at it every day. Top up the water when necessary. At first the seed swells as it takes in water. Then the seed splits and the root pops out and grows downwards. Very soon, the shoot will appear and grow upwards, reaching for the Sun. In a few days, the first leaves will appear, and you can leave the jar in sunlight. Having used the food stored in the seed, the young plant can now make its own food using sunlight.

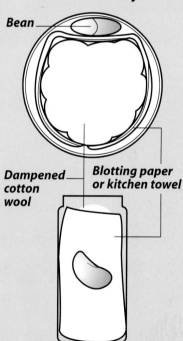

Bird's-eye view of the bean in the jar

Bean

Dampened cotton wool

Blotting paper or kitchen towel

Side view of the bean in the jar

15

Try this! Flower power

You will need a flower, a small sharp knife and a hand lens. Take a flower and, with an adult's help, slice carefully along its length. Use the hand lens to see the petals, the anthers, the sticky stigma and the ovary. Try the same thing with a piece of fruit, such as an apple. In the centre are the seeds, surrounded by the fleshy fruit.

Animal Life

What do fluffy rabbits, scary snakes, and biting fleas have in common? They're all animals – and so are we. But what makes an animal an animal and not a plant? Well, most of us animals move around and don't sit in the same place all the time like a tree (except when we're watching TV). We all eat things. And most animals can see what's happening around them. A great advantage if you want to find food and avoid nasty surprises.

What a lot there is

If you went for a swim and met a blue whale, you would never forget it. Well, it is 25 times longer than you. But if a tiny plankton animal floated past, you would totally ignore it. Not because you are rude, but because it is too small to see! Between the biggest and the smallest, there is so much animal life to be seen. Scientists have identified and named over one and a half million different species of animals but this is only part of the story. There may be 30, 50 or even an incredible 100 million species of animals yet to be discovered. So you'd better start looking, they may name a new species after you!

16

Chameleons change colour in response to factors such as temperature and light and emotions such as fright.

Did you know?

It's a dangerous world out there. There are plenty of hungry predators just waiting to pounce and sink their teeth into passing prey. So it's hardly surprising that animals need to defend themselves. Here are some of the ways they do it.

▶▶ Hide. Blend in with your surroundings, and no one can see you – in theory. That's what the crafty chameleon does. It actually changes colour.

▶▶ Run. This is what you would probably do to escape the toothy attentions of a passing crocodile or lion. But you wouldn't be able to catch a high-speed hare or overtake an ostrich.

▶▶ Disable the predator. Two tiny 'bags' in the skunk's bottom work just like water pistols. They squirt a stinking, stinging liquid into an attacker's face, leaving their opponent temporarily blinded and very, very smelly.

Vertebrates and invertebrates

The animals we know about fall into two clear groups called vertebrates and invertebrates. To join the vertebrate club you need to have a backbone and an inside skeleton. Members include fish, amphibians, reptiles, birds and mammals. You may be surprised to know that most species don't have a backbone. Animals in this group are called invertebrates, and members include sea anemones which remain fixed to the spot while they catch anything that floats past with their tentacles, earthworms that stretch and shorten to push their way through the soil, and insects, such as beetles, which have hard, outside skeletons.

Is there life in soil?

Try this!

You will need a small glass jar, a plastic funnel, an anglepoise lamp, a handful of soil and a hand lens. Garden soil looks pretty dull and lifeless, but it is really teeming with tiny animals. To see them, put the funnel into the top of the jar and the soil into the funnel. Position a desk lamp so that its bulb is 30cm above the funnel. Switch the lamp on and leave it for about an hour. Any animals in the soil will escape downwards, away from the heat and light, into the jar. Now, tip the contents of the jar into a glass dish. Look at it through a hand lens. See how many different animal types there are (and then return them safely back to the soil).

17

Amazing fact

Damp, dark and spooky caves are home to all sorts of weird and wonderful animals that never see the Sun. One of the oddest is the olm. This distant cousin of the frog doesn't need to see as it lives in total darkness. Nor does it need to have an attractive pattern on its skin because other olms can't see it!

Bones and Muscles

Tent poles are really useful. They make a framework to drape the tent fabric over, so that there's space inside to move around in and it doesn't fall down in the middle of the night. Bones do the same thing for an animal's body. The bony skeleton supports the body as well as protecting delicate bits inside like brains and lungs.

Muscle man

Stretched between the bones are muscles that give a body its basic shape and allow movement so that animals can run and jump. Muscles are unique. They are the only body tissues that can contract (get shorter) to pull bones and make the body move. But muscles can only pull, not push. So they are normally arranged in pairs.

18

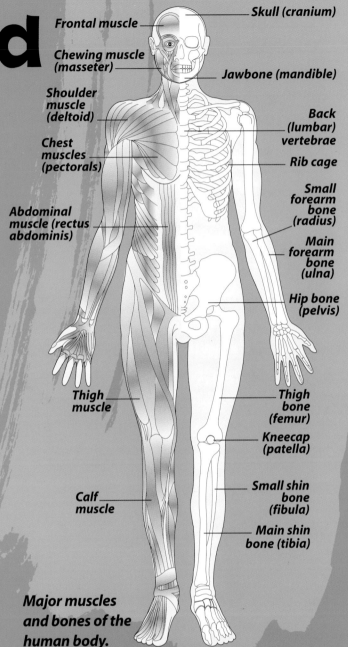

Frontal muscle

Skull (cranium)

Chewing muscle (masseter)

Jawbone (mandible)

Shoulder muscle (deltoid)

Back (lumbar) vertebrae

Chest muscles (pectorals)

Rib cage

Small forearm bone (radius)

Abdominal muscle (rectus abdominis)

Main forearm bone (ulna)

Hip bone (pelvis)

Thigh muscle

Thigh bone (femur)

Kneecap (patella)

Small shin bone (fibula)

Calf muscle

Main shin bone (tibia)

Major muscles and bones of the human body.

Moving around

How many different ways can you move? Most people can walk and run, just like lizards and leopards can (although sometimes we get out of breath). We can swim, but not with the same speed or style as a seal or a shark. To fly we need planes, unlike birds, bats, and insects. And, when it comes to hopping, we just can't keep up with frogs or kangaroos. As for sliding, it's best to leave that to snakes and slugs. The point is that animals move in many different ways. But from eels to elephants, animals generally move for the same reasons: to find food, avoid enemies (and relatives that turn up unexpectedly), and to find a mate.

Did you know?

Some animals make an annual journey – called migration – to breed, feed or escape the winter cold. The amazing Arctic tern is a bird that makes a migratory round trip of 32,000km each year. That's nearly seven times the distance from London to New York. It breeds in the Arctic in the summer, then flies south to the Antarctic to make the most of the southern hemisphere summer, then returns to the Arctic. Grey whales travel 18,000km each year when they move from the feeding areas in the Arctic to warmer breeding grounds off California – a journey of three months – before returning to the Arctic.

Try this! A snail's pace

You will need a snail and a piece of glass or a glass plate. Find out how snails are able to move without the benefit of owning legs. Find a garden snail and put it on a piece of glass. Wait until its head and foot (the flat, squidgy bit that it moves on) appear, then view the animal from underneath. You should be able to see rhythmic ridges ripple down the foot from front to back. These are made by contractions of muscles in the foot, and they push the mollusc slowly forward – at a snail's pace, of course.

Try this! Measuring muscles

You will need a tape measure. To investigate how two muscles work in opposite ways, roll up your sleeve and straighten your arm. Now, wrap the tape measure around your upper arm. Make a note of the measurement. Now, bend your arm, and measure again. You should find the size of your upper arm has increased. This is because the biceps muscle at the front of the upper arm has got fatter and shorter as it contracts to bend your arm. Now straighten your arm, You should feel the muscle at the back of your arm tighten slightly. This is the triceps muscle that straightens your arm. It does not bulge out as much as the biceps.

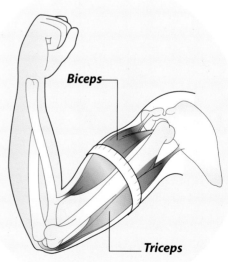

Biceps

Triceps

Brains and Behaviour

Sometimes, rather cruelly, you might describe someone as brainless. But if they really didn't have a brain they wouldn't be able to feel, move, see, or have a personality. Sitting cosily protected inside the skull, the brain controls just about everything going on inside the body.

Meerkats are intelligent community animals, working together and sharing duties such as watching for predators and hunting for food.

20

Brain power

Pinky-grey, and weighing about 1.5kg, your brain receives a constant stream of information from your eyes, ears, skin, nose, and tongue to tell it what is happening outside the body. It sorts all these messages out and compares them to earlier experiences. Then it sends out instructions, often to your muscles to move the body but also to other body bits. So, when you see a car racing towards you, your brain acts immediately and you jump out of the way. This is called behaviour. Making you feel sad, happy, angry, tired or hungry is also part of the brain's job. It makes you unique: there's no-one else quite like you.

Measuring reaction time

Try this! You will need a stopwatch or a watch that shows seconds and six other people. This simple experiment allows you to work out how long it takes you to react to something. Ask the six people to stand in a line, with their eyes closed and hold hands. Squeeze the hand of the first person and start the stopwatch at the same time. As soon as one person's hand is squeezed, they squeeze the hand of the next person, who squeezes the hand of the next person and so on down the line. When the last person feels their hand being squeezed they shout, and you stop the watch. Write down the number of seconds from start to finish and divide the number by six. That will tell how long, on average, it takes one person to react to something.

Try this!
Rapid reflexes

Reflex actions happen really quickly without you noticing. Many of them protect you from danger, like pulling your hand away automatically from something sharp or hot. Try this one out on a friend. Get them to stand in front of you, and look at their eyes. Without warning, clap your hands in front of their face (be careful not to touch them). What happens? They should blink immediately. Why? Because when something unusual happens in front of the eyes, the eyelids close by reflex to stop anything harming the eyes.

21

Changing personality

One way in which scientists can find out about how brains work is by studying people whose brains have been damaged. A classic example is the grisly case of an American man called Phineas Gage. In 1848, Phineas was setting a charge to blow up some rocks. A spark set off the explosion too soon, and drove an iron rod into his cheek, through the front part of his brain, and out of the top of his head. Ouch! The good news was that he survived. And the bad news: he was a changed man. Before the accident Phineas has been kind, polite and hard-working. After the accident he was bad-tempered and unreliable. But Phineas's misfortune made scientists realize for the first time that our personalities are controlled by the front part of our brain.

Area of the brain that controls speech

White matter (nerve fibres)

Part of the brain that controls movement

Part of the brain used in vision

Area of the brain that controls conscious thought

Cerebellum (controls muscles and balance)

Spinal cord

The inside of the human brain.

Making Sense

How dangerous life would be if you couldn't see where you were going, or if your house had caught fire and you couldn't smell the smoke. How boring it would be if you couldn't hear your stereo, or if foods such as chocolate and peaches had no taste. How strange it would seem if you couldn't feel heat or cold – you wouldn't have to wear a coat when you went out to play. Using our senses is a necessary part of survival for all animals.

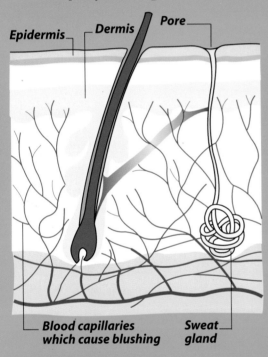

Epidermis Dermis Pore

Blood capillaries which cause blushing

Sweat gland

In touch

A living overcoat sounds a bit creepy, but that's exactly what you've got covering your body. Yes, it's skin we're talking about. It's waterproof to stop water soaking into the body and germproof to stop nasty bugs from getting in. It also gets darker in the sun to stop harmful rays from reaching the bottom layer. The skin has a fantastic collection of sensors for touch, pressure, pain, heat and cold, so you can experience the pleasures of touching a slimy slug, getting squashed on the bus or standing on a nail.

Seeing is believing

Finding your favourite food, checking out the latest fashions and watching a film all need eyes. Your eyes are light detectors. Whenever light hits them – which is all the time when you have your eyes open – they send messages to the back of the brain. Just like doing a jigsaw puzzle, your brain puts all the bits of information together so you actually 'see' whatever you're looking at.

Did you know?

For some animals, their sense of smell is of vital importance. With a nose at least ten times more sensitive than ours, dogs inhabit a world of smells far beyond human reach. Take a dog for a walk and it will sniff everything in sight from tree trunks to doggy bottoms, to give it a full 'smell picture' of its surroundings. Humans make the most of this canine ability – sniffer dogs are used to find drugs at airports or bloodhounds to follow a criminal's scent.

22

Sound detectors

What do you and elephants have, but sharks and rattlesnakes don't? The answer is ears. Ears are great for listening out for the rustling sounds made by food on the move, as well as for the terrifying approach of a hungry enemy.

If you drop a stone into water, you will see ripples move outwards from it. Sound waves travel though the air in much the same way. So, when you're daydreaming in class and your teacher shouts at you, his vibrating vocal cords will send pressure waves through the air to be picked up by your ears.

Elephants use their ears not only for hearing but also to regulate their body temperature.

Aromas and flavours

Smell and taste are really useful senses. And they work together to let you enjoy the flavours of food and drinks. But how do taste and smell actually work? Both depend on sensors that can detect chemicals. On your tongue are lots of small bumps called papillae.

Tucked down the side of these papillae are tiny sensors called taste buds. As for smell, through the nostrils and high up in the nasal passages (where no finger can reach) is a patch of smell sensors that pick up chemicals floating past in the air that you breathe in.

23

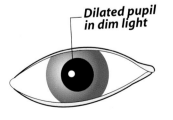

Automatic pupils

Small pupil in bright light

You will need a hand mirror. Use the mirror to look at your eyes. In the middle of each eye is a black dot called the pupil. This is actually a hole that lets light into the inside bit of the eye. Now go somewhere where the light is dim (but not complete darkness). Your pupils should get bigger, to let in as much light as possible. Now go somewhere bright. The pupils should get smaller, to stop the bright light damaging your eyes. Your pupil gets bigger and smaller automatically, without you having to think about it.

Dilated pupil in dim light

Food

As you've seen already, plants can make their own food just by sitting in the sun. No trips to the supermarket for them. Unfortunately you cannot. Two weeks lying on a holiday beach doesn't mean you can stop eating. You and other animals have actively to find food and eat it to give you energy and make you grow. Luckily, animals feed on all sorts of things, and feed in different ways so we are not all competing for the same thing.

24

Some herbivores live in groups so that they can feed and watch for danger at the same time.

Meat and two veg

Animals that just eat plants, such as cows, zebras and grasshoppers, are called herbivores. Wolves, sharks and other carnivores – or meat-eaters – need a nice piece of meat to keep them going. While omnivores, like people and pigs, will eat anything put in front of them, unless their parents say it's good for them (does not apply to pigs).

Food processing

Close your eyes and think about your favourite food. Imagine you are popping it into your mouth and enjoying the great flavours. Now think ahead a day or two. Does what comes out of your bottom smell or look as good? Well, we don't need to go into graphic details about this. It is enough to say that between one end and the other something has happened to the food. The only clues are a few burps, rumbles and farts. But what is really going on?

Did you know?

Snakes and other ectotherms, or 'cold-blooded animals', do not have to eat every day, unlike endotherms, or 'warm-blooded animals' such as dogs and humans. Ectotherms need far less energy from their food because they do not have to keep their bodies warm like we do. In fact, a dog needs so much energy that it has to eat ten times more than a snake of the same weight. And snakes can eat a large meal at one sitting and not have to eat again for weeks – imagine swallowing whole a hamburger twice your size. The downside for snakes, and other reptiles, is that they need to spend time basking in the sun to warm up their bodies before they become fully active. Humans like basking too, but only to get a suntan.

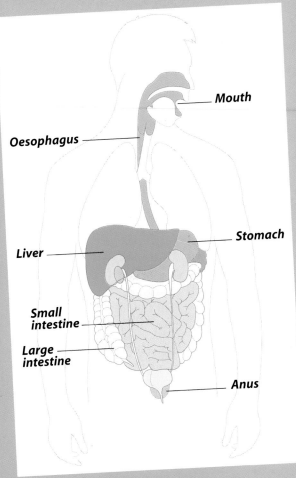

The human digestive system.

Top to bottom

Running from mouth (top opening) to anus (bottom opening) is a long tube called the digestive system. This is about 10m long but, fortunately, the longest bits – the intestines – are coiled up, otherwise you would need to be as tall as a house. You need food to give you energy and the raw materials to grow. Food is made up of big molecules that your body cannot use straight away, so your digestive system breaks down food into tiny molecules that the body can use. Crushed by the teeth, churned by the stomach, and attacked by chemical digesters called enzymes, food is soon reduced to the consistency of lumpy chicken soup. Useful stuff is soaked up through the intestines and into the bloodstream. Any leftover waste is dried out in the large intestine, and given a nice brown colour by waste blood cells and a charming smell by the friendly bacteria that live there. It's quite an amazing process.

25

Try this!

Teeth

You will need a hand-mirror. Take the mirror and, with your mouth open, hold it so that you can see your teeth. Humans have four types of teeth that make up a sort of digestive tool kit. Chisel-like incisor teeth at the front of the jaws cut food. Pointed canine teeth (longer in Dracula and other vampires) grip and pierce food. Flat premolars and molars at the back of the jaws grind and crush food. You have two sets of teeth during your lifetime. The first set – the milk teeth – start appearing when you are about 6 months old (usually accompanied by sore gums and loud crying). Eventually 24 milk teeth pop out through the gums, but from the age of 6 they are gradually replaced by the second set of permanent teeth that grow up from below. By the age of 18 or 20 you should have 32 teeth in place (if you avoid fighting or falling out of trees). Count how many teeth you have.

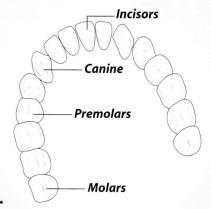

The Breath of Life

It doesn't matter whether you're a human or a hawk, an owl or a pussy cat, an ox or a parrot. Once you stop breathing permanently, that's it. You're dead. Breathing gets air into the body, and the oxygen in air is something that every living thing has to have to stay alive. Oxygen is essential to release energy locked in the food we eat. Energy powers everything we do from swooping on prey (owls) to running for the bus (you).

Lungs

In the case of humans and our relatives (other vertebrates, not just aunts and uncles), breathing moves air in and out of the bag-like lungs in the chest. From there, oxygen goes into the blood, which carries it to every single energy-hungry cell. A poisonous waste gas called carbon dioxide released by cells is carried back to the lungs and breathed out. Blood is pumped to the lungs to pick up oxygen and then round the rest of the body by the heart. This beats – contracts or squeezes – between 50 and 80 times every minute.

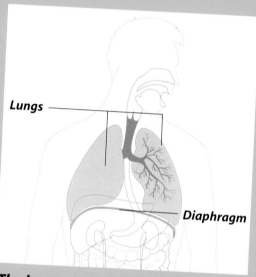

The human respiratory system.

Round and round

Four hundred years ago, no-one really knew how blood moved inside the body. The most popular idea – dating back thousands of years – was that it went up and down blood vessels, a bit like the tide going in and out. In 1628 all that changed. That was the year William Harvey – physician to King Charles I – showed that blood flows around the body in a closed loop. It travels away from the heart along arteries and back to the heart along veins. Most important of all, he demonstrated this by doing proper experiments – just like you do in school science – instead of guessing, like most other people did then.

William Harvey (1578–1657) proved that the heart pumped blood around the body.

Try this!

How fast is your heart?

You will need a watch with a second hand. Find your pulse by putting two fingers together on the inside of your wrist, just below your thumb. Each pulse represents one beat of your heart. Count the number of pulse beats for ten seconds. Multiply them by six, and you will get your heart rate in beats per minute. Now run on the spot for two minutes. Repeat the pulse count. You should discover that your heart is beating faster. Why? Because your muscles are working harder, and they need more blood to bring them extra food and oxygen.

Try this!

Steamy breath

You will need a small hand mirror. Take the mirror and breathe on to it. It should go cloudy just like the bathroom mirror when you are having a bath. This is because when you breathe out, you are not only expelling carbon dioxide, but also small water droplets. These come from the moist insides of your lungs.

Amazing fact

There are over 100,000km of blood vessels inside you. The main blood vessels which take blood away from the heart are called arteries and the main blood vessels that carry it back to the heart are called veins. In between, there are lots and lots of tiny blood capillaries which connect all parts of the body.

27

Did you know?

How long can you hold your breath? One minute? Perhaps a little more? Dolphins can hold their breath for over 15 minutes while they dive for food. Mammals like us, dolphins take in oxygen from the air through blowholes on top of their heads and they are able to slow down their hearts so that oxygen is pumped around their bodies more slowly.

Generating Genes

One thing is certain in life: we all have to die sometime. Fortunately, we and our fellow living organisms have a neat replacement service to make sure someone is there to take over. It's called reproduction. For humans, and many other animals, to reproduce, two individuals belonging to different sexes – male and female – have to get together. This is known as sexual reproduction.

Your genes

Inside every cell in a body is a set of 46 chromosomes. These are long strings made out of massive molecules called DNA, divided up into handy chunks called genes. Your 100,000 or so genes contain all the instructions needed to make you look human but also to give you a few unique features. Back to sexual reproduction – men and women produce tiny packages, each carrying 23 chromosomes. The male package is the fast-moving sperm, while the female is the slow-moving, larger egg. If egg and sperm meet, the packages unite, and 46 chromosomes get cracking on making a new human which pops out from its mother some nine months later.

Try this!

Whorls and loops

You will need an ink pad and a piece of plain paper. The ridges on your fingers are really useful because they help you grip things when you pick them up. You can examine them by making prints of them, called fingerprints. Roll your left thumb on the pad, then roll it on to the paper. Repeat with each of your left fingers, and then your right thumb and fingers. Make a note in each case of which finger is which. If you look at each fingerprint you will see it is made up of a pattern. This may be a whorl, a loop, an arch, or a composite – a mixture of the other three. All your fingerprints will be different. And no two people's fingerprints are the same, not even identical twins (who share exactly the same genes). That's because fingerprints are not controlled by genes, but by conditions experienced by a baby inside its mother. Your finger markings grow as you grow but their characteristic shape doesn't change.

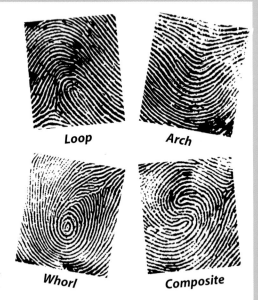

Loop

Arch

Whorl

Composite

Animals' markings demonstrate their unique genes.

Did you know?

Apart from identical twins, everyone has a unique set of genes, so yours are different from your parents, your brothers and sisters and your friends, even if you look or act just like them. The same is true for most animals and some plants. Next time you pass a field of cows or sheep, see if you can tell the difference between each one – it's not always easy!

 **Tongue rollers**

Collect a group of friends and see how many of them can roll their tongue. Tongue rolling is something that people can either do or not do – they can't half do it. The ability to tongue roll – or not – is controlled by just two genes and inherited by children from their parents. Very often, if one parent can roll his or her tongue, the children will be able to as well.

29

Unravelling DNA

One of the great scientific discoveries of the last century was the structure of DNA. It meant that scientists could find out exactly how features were passed on from parents to children. Now, at the beginning of the 21st century, research has progressed so much that scientists have identified all the DNA making up the genes in human chromosomes. The great breakthrough was made in 1953 by American James Watson and Englishman Francis Crick. Using information gleaned by another scientist called Rosalind Franklin, they managed to build a model of DNA. It was called a double helix, and looked like a twisted ladder. This was a great leap forward for biology.

A model of the DNA molecule containing human genes.

Growing Up

Whoever you are, your life follows the same sort of pattern. For the first 20 years you grow and develop, and then growth stops. The same is true of other mammals and of birds – but not of reptiles, they grow throughout their life.

It's just a phase

Growth goes through different phases. Babies from birth to one year old grow really fast. Through childhood you grow steadily, with your bones getting longer, thicker and stronger. Then, between the ages of 10 and 13 (earlier in girls than boys) things really change. You suddenly get bigger and your body changes shape so it looks more like a grown-up. You start to think differently as well – this might mean a few arguments with parents but it's perfectly normal. By the age of 20, the process is complete and, with luck, the arguments are over.

30

Try this! Changing height

Use a pencil and a tape measure to measure your height and that of your friends. To do this, find a suitable wall that you can make markings on (ask permission first). Put a friend against the wall and mark the position of the top of their head on the wall with the pencil. Repeat this with your other friends, and get someone to do it for you. Do this every month – are you growing?

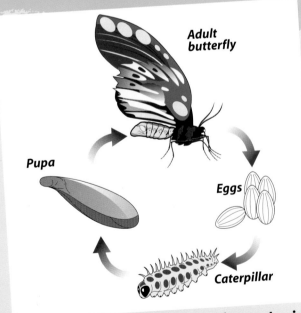

The four stages of butterfly metamorphosis.

Did you know?

Growing up can be more dramatic for insects than it is for humans. The trouble with insects is that their skeletons are on the outside, not the inside. That means they must 'shed' their skeletons every so often, allowing the insects to grow rapidly before their new outer skins have hardened again. This transformation is called metamorphosis. Other insects, such as butterflies, travel a different route. Their eggs hatch into caterpillars that trundle around eating lots and shedding their skins. Then they rest up for a while as a pupa to reorganize themselves, finally emerging as a beautiful butterfly.

Glossary

Bacteria
Microscopic organisms which are each made up of one cell.

Carnivore
Animal which eats only meat.

Cell
The structural unit which makes up all living things.

Classification
To arrange something in order or in groups.

Community
A group of animals and plants living in the same place.

Decomposer
Animal or plant which breaks down dead matter.

Digestion
Breaking down food into small particles to be absorbed into the bloodstream.

DNA
Main chemical making up the genetic material of all living things.

Ecosystem
Community of plants and animals and their surrounding habitat.

Food chain
Animals and plants which are linked together because one eats another.

Food web
A number of food chains which are connected.

Genus
A group of species which share similar features.

Germination
Growth of a plant from a seed.

Habitat
Natural living place of an animal or plant.

Herbivore
Animal which eats only plants.

Invertebrate
An animal without a backbone, such as insects and worms.

Omnivore
Animal which eats both meat and plants.

Organisms
A living thing, made up of one or more cells.

Photosynthesis
The process by which plants use sunlight to make food.

Reproduction
The process by which new members of an animal or plant species are created.

Skeleton
The framework of bones that support the human body.

Species
A group of animals or plants which breed together.

Vertebrate
An animal with a backbone, such as birds, mammals and most fish.

31

Index